LESSONS IN LIFE

by

TRACEY WOLFFE

An A-Z of uplifting, positive aphorisms, illustrated throughout by the author's colourful, inspirational artwork:

www.traceywolffe.co.uk

Copyright © 2011 Tracey Wolffe

All rights reserved. No part of this publication may be reproduced or transmitted in any form or by any means, electronic or mechanical including photocopying, recording or any information storage or retrieval system, without prior permission in writing from the publishers.

The right of Tracey Wolffe to be identified as the author of this work has been asserted by her in accordance with the Copyright, Designs and Patents Act 1988

First published in the United Kingdom in 2011 by
HEARTWORK PUBLISHING

Reprinted in 2018

ISBN 978-0-9571047-0-9

Cover painting by Tracey Wolffe:
Life

For my beautiful rainbow children, Nathan Jamie and Daniella Rose

with love
Tracey x

Angels Fly Because They Take Themselves Lightly!

ALLOW yourself to relax, smile, laugh, and have some fun!

Ease up on yourself

Stop blaming and criticising yourself

Homeland

BEAUTY pervades the natural world

Be aware; and appreciate the wondrous variety of colours, forms, sounds and scents

Creativity

CREATIVITY is fulfilling and life-giving

Bake, make, grow, arrange, design, paint, write!

Bubbles

Nathan

FORGIVE others, and yourself

Learn, and move on

The Storm is Over

Exercise is a natural and exhilarating way to regulate and release the physical body

Dance, stretch, walk, run, play!

High Energy

DISCRIMINATE in who and what is good for you

Define your personal boundaries

Know your limits

Protect your energy

GROWTH is the essence of life

The challenges we encounter are designed to help us learn and grow

Be prepared to change and evolve

Unity

HEALTH is harmony of mind, body and soul

I'm Every Woman!

INTUITION is a precious gift

Connect with it, and listen to it at all times

Do what feels right for you

Make your own choices

Be your own guru!

Contrasts

Peace

LOVE is the most powerful, healing force in the universe

Generate unconditional love in your heart for yourself, and all beings

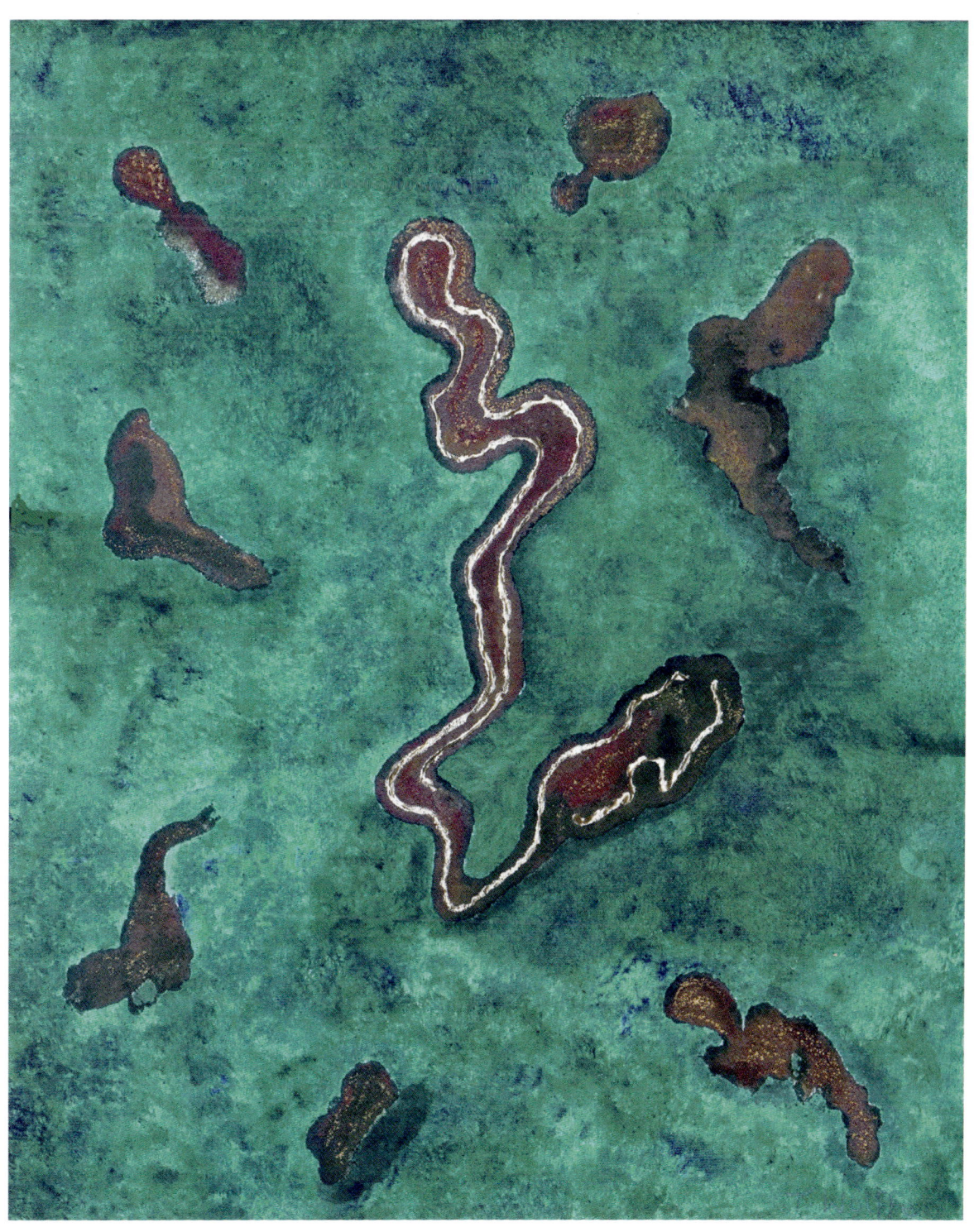

Sea of Love

KINDNESS to others brings its own reward

Be kind to yourself

Dolphin Heart

Joy lifts the heart and mind

Surround yourself with beauty, music, laughter, and wonderful beings

MINDFULNESS brings peace

Relax the body, breath and mind

Find the quietness within

Open up to inspiration and guidance

Dolphin Love

NURTURE yourself and others

Be kind, patient, gentle and understanding

Stream of Consciousness

Observe your THOUGHTS

Keep them positive, light and loving

Expect the best

Dwell on the good things in life

Recognise the power of the mind to manifest reality

Heartsong

PURSUE your GOALS with enthusiasm and commitment

Make your dreams come true!

Balance

QUALITY of LIFE involves a balance between activity and stillness; company and solitude

Natural Woman

Respect your Body

Fuel it with fresh nutritious food that makes it fit and strong

Heal it with rest

Listen to what it is telling you

Pace yourself

Thank it for what it enables you to do, and love it

Into the Light

SHARE in life's abundance

Give generously and more will come your way

Focus on your blessings, not your lack

Your needs will always be met

Allow yourself to feel that you deserve to receive, and succeed

Heartbreak

TRUST, relax, and let go of fear and anxiety

Maintain faith and hope

Know that you can deal with any situation

Into the Deep

Understand yourself

Utilise your strengths for the highest good of all

Be the best that you can be

Vocalise

Voice your point of view calmly

Be centred at all times

Be true to yourself

Suppression

WELLBEING is enhanced by really feeling your emotions as they arise, without self-castigation; then releasing and letting them go

These Boots

These Boots

WELLBEING is enhanced by really feeling your emotions as they arise, without self-castigation; then releasing and letting them go

X-RAY VISION of the motivation and path of another is not within our gift

Try not to judge others

Let them follow their own path

Don't take their behaviour personally

Sunshine

You are a special and unique person

Everything that you need is within you

Be strong, independent, self-nurturing, self-sustaining

Believe in yourself!

Fireworks

ZEST for **LIFE** is the key to success

It keeps the old young, and the sick alive

Give thanks, and make the most of every day

Enjoy life to the full

BIOGRAPHY

Tracey Wolffe (née Gold) was born in Scotland, and has lived most of her life in England, with sojourns in Brussels as an au pair, and Paris as a lawyer.

Her career has been extremely varied. After her law degree at Balliol College, Oxford University, she qualified at Clifford Chance as a corporate lawyer, with First Class Honours from the Law Society. She went on to become a Law Tutor to graduates and undergraduates at Bournemouth University, as well as developing state of the art computer-based legal courseware, whilst qualifying and practising as a BWY yoga teacher. She has studied homeopathy, nutrition, and naturopathy, and became a professional artist at the start of the new millennium.

Tracey is a devoted mother to two beautiful young children, the first of whom was born with brain damage. She has become a mother tiger for him, using new-found strength, together with all the skills she has developed over her lifetime, to fight for his wellbeing.

Her life has, in the last 3 decades, been full of enormous challenges, balanced by many gifts and blessings.

Tiger Tiger